ALTERNATOR BOOKS™

WATER IS LIFE

The Ongoing Fight for Indigenous Water Rights

KATRINA M. PHILLIPS

Lerner Publications ◆ Minneapolis

To Leo and Max

Content consultant: Matthew J. Martinez

Lerner Publications Company
An imprint of Lerner Publishing Group, Inc.
241 First Avenue North
Minneapolis, MN 55401 USA

For reading levels and more information, look up this title at www.lernerbooks.com.

Main body text set in Aptifer Sans LT Pro Medium.
Typeface provided by Linotype AG.

Designer: Athena Currier **Photo Editor:** Nicole Berglund
Lerner team: Brianna Kaiser, Sue Marquis

Map illustration on page 24 by Laura K. Westlund.

Library of Congress Cataloging-in-Publication Data

Names: Phillips, Katrina M., author.
Title: Water is life : the ongoing fight for indigenous water rights / Katrina M. Phillips.
Description: Minneapolis : Lerner Publications, [2025] | Series: Native rights (Alternator Books) | Includes bibliographical references and index. | Audience: Ages 8–12 | Audience: Grades 4–6 | Summary: "For many Indigenous peoples, water is not just important to drink. It is also sacred. Learn how Indigenous peoples around the world are fighting for their rights to use and protect the water we all share"—Provided by publisher.
Identifiers: LCCN 2024010826 (print) | LCCN 2024010827 (ebook) | ISBN 9798765646939 (library binding) | ISBN 9798765661727 (paperback) | ISBN 9798765656792 (epub)
Subjects: LCSH: Indians of North America—Government relations—Juvenile literature. | Water rights—United States—Juvenile literature. | Indians of North America—Legal status, laws, etc.—Juvenile literature.
Classification: LCC E93 .P53 2025 (print) | LCC E93 (ebook) | DDC 346.04/3208997—dc23/eng/20240326

LC record available at https://lccn.loc.gov/2024010826
LC ebook record available at https://lccn.loc.gov/2024010827

Manufactured in the United States of America
1-1010988-53134-5/2/2024

TABLE OF CONTENTS

INTRODUCTION
WATER PROTECTORS

In 2016 Indigenous peoples began protesting the building of the Dakota Access Pipeline (DAPL). The oil pipeline would cross over North Dakota, South Dakota, Iowa, and Illinois. Many people of the Standing Rock Sioux Tribe and the Cheyenne River Sioux Tribe were afraid the DAPL would endanger their lands and water sources.

The protesters began calling themselves water protectors and using the motto Mní Wičóni, meaning "water is life." They argued that the DAPL would cut them off from their sacred sites. And if the DAPL ever leaked, it would pollute the clean water on their land.

The water protectors set up camps to stop the DAPL from being built. After nearly a year of protests, the US National Guard forced the last of the water protectors and their supporters from the camps. The DAPL finished construction

Tusweca Mendoza and members of the Standing Rock Sioux Tribe attend the 2016 protest of the Dakota Access Pipeline held in Virginia.

in 2017. But the water protectors made people around the world pay attention to water rights.

Many Indigenous peoples in the US have limited access to clean water. Indigenous households are nineteen times more likely than non-Indigenous households to lack indoor plumbing. And the Navajo, who call themselves Diné, are sixty-seven times more likely than other people in the US to live without running water.

Indigenous peoples continue fighting for their rights to water. As climate change makes clean water harder to access in many parts of the US, the work of water protectors is more important than ever.

CHAPTER 1
Stories of Water

Water has always been important to Indigenous peoples. For many, water is sacred. For some, it is the place of their creation. The creation stories of Indigenous peoples reflect the importance of water in their cultures as a source for all living things.

Creation Stories

The creation story of the Dakota in what is now Minnesota tells how people were first created at Bdote. Bdote means "where two waters come together." It's where the waters of

Bdote, the place where the Mni Sota Wakpa and Wakpa Tanka meet

the Minnesota River (Mni Sota Wakpa) and the Mississippi River (Wakpa Tanka) meet.

In the Ojibwe creation story, only a few animals survived a great flood. The animals thought they could dive down into the water to find some mud to create a new world. When each animal tried, they could not dive down far enough.

A little muskrat was the last to try. After a long time, he came to the surface with some mud in his paw. The animals spread the mud on the turtle's back, which became the earth.

Megan Toben participating in a 2016 water ceremony at the Oceti Sakowin Camp

Using Water

Indigenous peoples have used water in different ways depending on where they live or have lived. Indigenous peoples on the coasts fished in lakes and hunted in the oceans. Heavy rainfall helped Indigenous peoples in the Southeast grow crops such as corn, beans, squash, and sweet potatoes.

REFLECT

Many Indigenous peoples historically relied on water for resources and travel. How do you think changes in water rights affected where these peoples lived?

The Seminole lived in chickees in the Everglades. These houses are built on stilts. The Ojibwe living near Lake Superior (Gichigami) have harvested wild rice in freshwater lakes for centuries.

Harvey Goodsky Jr. (*left*) and Morningstar Goodsky harvest wild rice on Rice Lake in Minnesota in 2017.

Think about everything you use water for each day. Why is having access to water important?

In the drier lands of the Southwest, Indigenous peoples learned how to manage their water use. Indigenous peoples built ditches, dams, canals, and water storage systems in the lands of Utah, Arizona, Nevada, California, and New Mexico. Some, like the Tongva, chose places to live based on how many people the local rivers could support.

CHAPTER 2
Life in the West

Water is an important resource, especially in places such as the Southwest where the land is dry and arid. Finding water sources isn't always easy. There are often arguments about who can use the water and how much of it they can use.

Farmers' Journey West

Farmers from the eastern US began moving to the West in the 1800s. The US government promised farmland at low prices or for free.

Congress passed the Oregon Donation Land Act in 1850 to encourage more people to settle in the West. Within the next five years, more than nine thousand settlers claimed almost 3 million acres (1.2 million ha) of Indigenous land. The Homestead Act of 1862 promised 160 acres (65 ha) of free land to anyone who could farm it for at least five years. Close to four million people claimed land through this act.

A woodcut of a farmer in the 1800s

A family of settlers on farmland in Nebraska after President Abraham Lincoln signed the Homestead Act of 1862

Ranchers and farmers needed lots of water to raise animals and grow crops. They claimed much of the water that Indigenous peoples were using for their own needs. They also dug channels for irrigation. Channels move water from one place to another.

Claiming Indigenous Land and Water

These lands in the West were Indigenous lands. To get access to the water on these lands, the US government forced many Indigenous peoples to sign treaties. These treaties forced Indigenous peoples off their homelands with water access and onto much smaller pieces of land called reservations. Many of these reservations were built on lands that weren't good for farming.

This is the Navajo (Diné) Treaty of 1868. Part of the treaty allowed the Diné to return to their ancestral homelands.

When Indigenous peoples built dams and canals, they always made sure to leave water for others to use. They saw protecting land and water as part of their greater responsibility to the earth.

Many gold miners went to California in the 1800s, and gold mining used lots of water.

REFLECT

In the 1800s, waves of farmers and other settlers created higher demand for water in the West. How did this hurt Indigenous peoples and their access to water?

American settlers did not always hold the same beliefs. They saw land and water as goods to be used and sold. They ignored Indigenous practices of water use. And they often fought to keep water away from Indigenous lands.

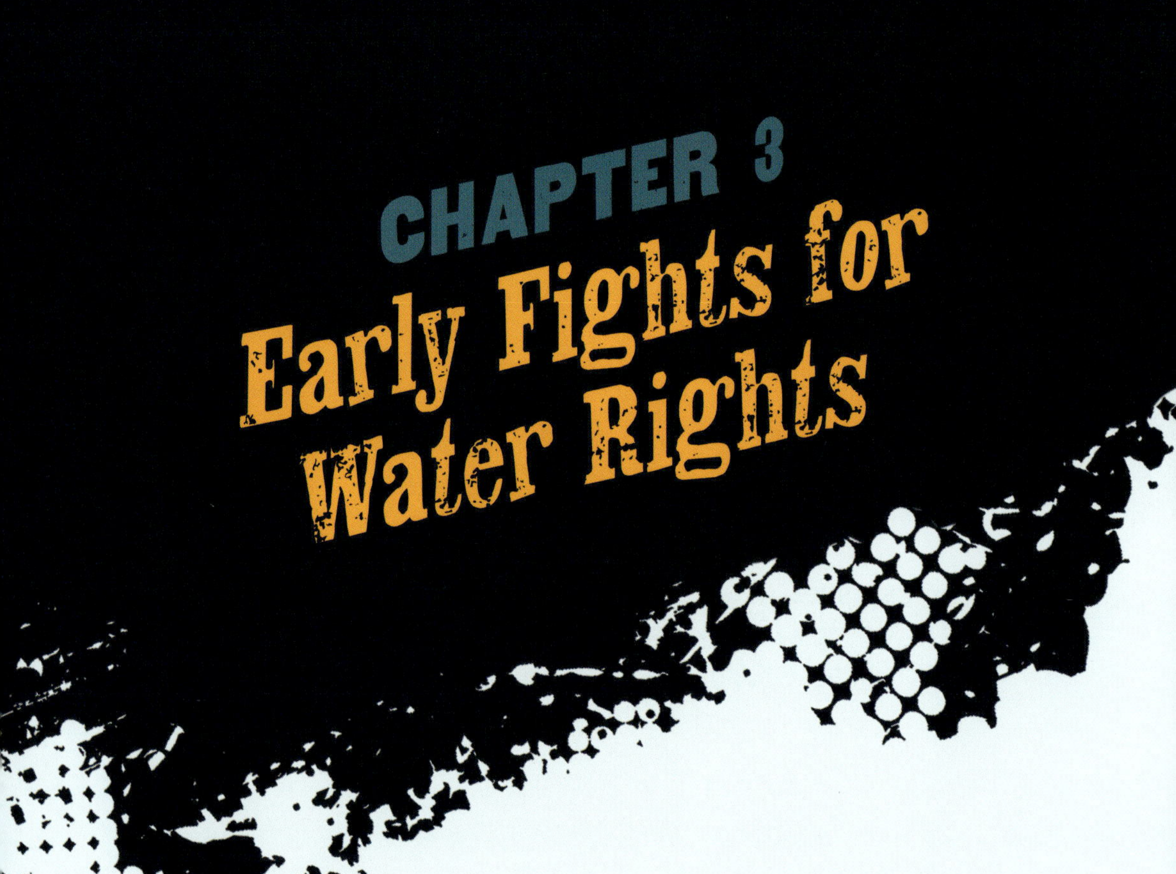

CHAPTER 3
Early Fights for Water Rights

As more settlers moved to the West, the government forced more Indigenous peoples from their homelands. Some homelands were prime for farming and herding. This included the homelands of the Diné.

The Long Walk

In the early 1860s, General James Carleton ordered Kit Carson to lead a campaign to force the Diné off their lands and onto a reservation in the Bosque Redondo. This campaign included destroying the water sources of the Diné.

The Diné were forcibly removed from their homelands and sent to Bosque Redondo in the 1860s.

In 1864 Carson's men began forcing the Diné to walk about 300 miles (483 km) to Bosque Redondo. Hundreds died on the journey, which became known as the Long Walk. The Diné did not have access to water or good foods on the reservation. Many more Diné died from disease or starvation after arriving there.

In 1868 the Diné signed a treaty with the US government that would allow them to return to their homelands. But they had a much smaller portion of homeland than they had before the Long Walk.

The Winters Doctrine

The Fort Belknap Indian Reservation was created by a treaty in 1888 as the new home for the Gros Ventre, who call themselves Aaniiih, and the Assiniboine, who call themselves Nakoda. The Milk River flowed through this land. But farmers who lived upstream changed the direction of the Milk River away from the reservation. When the US government told the farmers to return the river to its natural course, the farmers fought back.

Irene Rock of the Nakoda at the Fort Belknap Indian Reservation in the early 1900s

REFLECT

Do you think water access is a human right? Why or why not?

In 1908 the case made it to the Supreme Court. The Supreme Court ruled that the treaty that created the reservation gave rights to the Aaniiih and Nakoda to use the waters of the Milk River. This decision is known as the Winters Doctrine. It has protected Indigenous peoples' access to water for over a hundred years.

CHAPTER 4 The Fight Continues

The Colorado River has always been an important resource. The river is over 1,000 miles (1,600 km) long and is the main water source for forty million people. This includes the Indigenous peoples living in the Colorado River basin. The basin is in Arizona, California, Nevada, Colorado, New Mexico, Utah, and Wyoming.

There is often not enough water for the Indigenous peoples living near the Colorado River. And Indigenous peoples have often been excluded when the US or state governments have made choices about how to use the river's water.

In 1992 ten Indigenous nations formed the Ten Tribes Partnership. It formed to protect Indigenous peoples' use of the Colorado River. It also gives Indigenous peoples a voice in talks about how to use the river.

Horseshoe Bend of the Colorado River

NATIVE NATIONS AND WATER SOURCES IN ARIZONA

* This map shows federally recognized tribes in Arizona as of 2024. Indigenous land boundaries have shifted throughout history due to settlers.

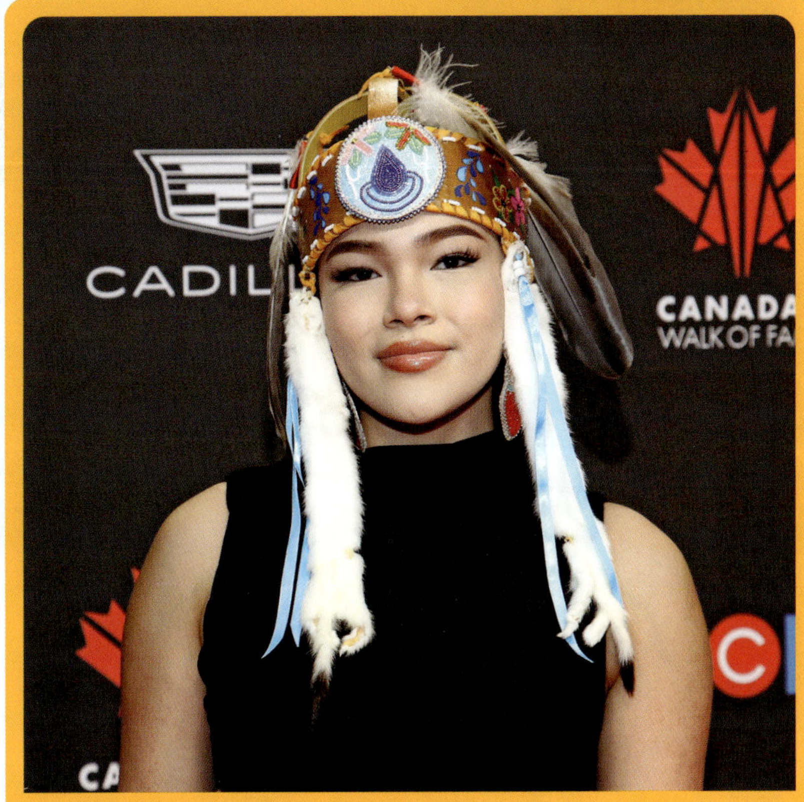

Autumn Peltier was named Canada's Walk of Fame 2023 Community Hero for her impact on her community.

Access to Clean Water

Many Indigenous peoples must fight to protect their clean water from pollution. Activist Autumn Peltier has been the chief water commissioner of the Anishinabek Nation since 2019. In 2016 Peltier, then twelve, gave Canadian prime minister Justin Trudeau a gift from the Anishinaabe during the Assembly of First Nations. She also criticized his clean-water policies. Since then Peltier has spoken in front of world leaders about clean drinking water for Indigenous peoples.

MORE RUNNING WATER

About 30 percent of Diné families don't have sinks or toilets. They often have to drive miles for running water and ration water for cooking, bathing, and washing. In 2014 the Navajo Water Project began. The Navajo Water Project brings running water to homes that don't have access to water or sewer lines. It has helped hundreds of families in New Mexico, Utah, and Arizona.

Otto Tso, Latoya Nez, and Arya Richardson fill up a water tank at a watering station on the Navajo Nation in 2021.

In 2016 women of the Yurok Tribe and California governor Jerry Brown attend a ceremony to sign the amended Klamath Hydroelectric Settlement Agreement, which discusses the removal of four dams on the Klamath River.

Indigenous peoples across the West have spent decades fighting for the removal of dams. Dams are often used to collect water or create energy, but they also make big changes to the environment. They can destroy fish and wildlife populations or prevent water from reaching Indigenous peoples downstream. Removing the dams can help bring back fish populations and help more Indigenous peoples have access to clean water.

Thanks to Indigenous activists, the US government agreed to start removing four dams along the Klamath River in 2023. The river runs through Oregon and California. Indigenous peoples hope the removal of the dams will restore the river and bring back the salmon populations.

PROTECTING WATER SUPPLIES

Nicole Horseherder is a founding member of Tó Nizhóní Ání, which means "sacred water speaks." Horseherder, who is Diné, helped form the organization in 2001 after learning that coal mining operations were draining 3 to 4 million gallons (11 to 15 million L) of water a day from a local water source Indigenous peoples needed to access. Local residents were also being exposed to dangerous coal dust. Horseherder and Tó Nizhóní Ání were able to end the mining operations.

The Copco 2 Dam on the Klamath River, shown here in 2009, was fully removed in 2023.

Indigenous peoples around the world continue to fight for their people, their lands, and their ways of life. By protecting rivers, lakes, and oceans, they are protecting the environment and fighting for a better future for everyone.

Glossary

activist: a person who campaigns for social change

arid: a very dry area with little rainfall

campaign: a series of actions to bring about a result

climate change: a change in the temperatures and usual weather in a particular place, caused by humans and the burning of fossil fuels

culture: the beliefs, customs, and languages of a group of people

irrigation: the practice of creating human-made channels to help move water over land to grow crops

policy: a law or method of action by a government

reservation: in the US, an area of land held and governed by Native nations. There are more than three hundred reservations in the US.

treaty: an official document signed between two or more sovereign nations

water rights: rights to use water, often provided by treaties with the US or Canadian governments

Learn More

American Museum of Natural History: What Is Water?
https://www.amnh.org/explore/ology/water/what-is-water

Garré, Sarah, and Marijke Huysmans. *The Wonderful World of Water: From Dams to Deserts*. New York: Prestel, 2023.

Knutson, Julie. *Do the Work! Climate Action, Life below Water, and Life on Land*. Ann Arbor, MI: Cherry Lake, 2022.

Navajo Water Project
https://www.navajowaterproject.org

NOAA: Dams on the West Coast
https://www.fisheries.noaa.gov/west-coast/endangered-species-conservation/dams-west-coast

Phillips, Katrina M. *Indigenous Environmentalism: Honoring Our Relationships and Responsibilities with Nature*. Minneapolis: Lerner Publications, 2025.

Smithsonian: American Indian Responses to Environmental Challenges
https://americanindian.si.edu/environment/

Walker, Tracy Sue. *Climate Change Activism*. Minneapolis: Lerner Publications, 2023.

Index

Photo Acknowledgments

Image credits: AP Photo/Pablo Martinez Monsivais, p. 5; Nature and Science/Alamy, p. 7; AP Photo/David Goldman, p. 8; Star Tribune/Getty Images, p. 10; North Wind Picture Archives/Alamy, p. 13; Bettmann/Getty Images, p. 14; AP Photo/Paul Morigi/AP Images for National Museum of the American Indian, p. 15; Kathy deWitt/Alamy, p. 16; National Archives Catalog, p. 19; Heritage Image Partnership Ltd/Alamy, p. 20; Enrique Aguirre Aves/Getty Images, p. 23; Jeremy Chan/Stringer/Getty Images, p. 25; The Washington Post/Getty Images, p. 26; AP Photo/Will Houston/The Times-Standard, p. 27; AP Photo/Jeff Barnard, p. 29.

Cover: mikesj11/Shutterstock; Archiwiz/Shutterstock; Save nature and wildlife/Shutterstock; Miloje/Shutterstock; Northern Owl/Shutterstock; Kiwihug/Unsplash.